A King In Us

Poems from the country of many Gods and beyond

Adity Karki

BookLeaf
Publishing

India | USA | UK

Made with ❤ on the BookLeaf Publishing Platform
www.bookleafpub.in
www.bookleafpub.com

Dedication

Dedicated
to all those
who are healed
by their writing.

Preface

I am grateful for the existence of poetry in my life. From an early age, it has been the medicine of my pain. It allows me to peek into the absurdity of human emotions. It allows me to visit the stigmatized zones in my interpersonal relationships with family, friends and strangers. When in heavy distress, I literally write, dear poems come to me for the rescue. The knowledge brought by poems have shown me the path to freedom, and they keep showing me that it might be a life long journey of freeing oneself from the traps of the decay in the collectives I am surrounded by. Sharing medicine is a vulnerable act because it tells others of the disease you are treating. But there is comfort in knowing that diseases are never of just one person. May my poems free the traps of shame and gaze. My best wishes to them.

Acknowledgements

I would have never made the first attempt to push for my poetry book. BookLeaf publishing I thank you for this challenge, and support to publish. My first ever published book ! I express my sincere gratitude to the people in the team. Thank you for making this happen.

1

The undiagnosed me

Ding Ding Ding
Doeing Doeing Doeing
This or That !
Which first?
Oh no, how about that one!
Eyes saw this too, so that now
Ding Ding Ding
Another thought !
Doeing Doeing Doeing
A different one! again in my mind.

Time has gone pass by but ding ding ding
Doeing Doeing.
Frozeeeeeeeen.
Dinnngggggggg.
Doeiiimfkzukil..hang.

Ding Ding Ding Doeing Doeing Doeing
Ding Ding Ding Doeing Doeing Doeing

2

Gratitude to the Rappers

If you don't rap, if you know only to please
Where will you puke all the filth?
That accumulates, but you know only to please
No bars to spit, all the hatred and disgust of the collapse
of the world
So much filth, where will you spill?

Chains in your hands, bondage of the age, dreams that
materials braid
All that is dying you see, and all that is left behind is
numbed and aspirational of only the individual
No choices it seems,
How much do I run?
Away from the family of which I no longer speak
the same language-
either you are a baggage now, or are they!
Away to find another collective
Away from the patterns that dissolve me
Away to explore another high

Away but never spitting those bars that accumulates,
all the hatred for the things that made you run, if you
don't spit, where will you spill?

The addictions that run through generations
The outrage of being violated and never spoken of
The labor that your women accumulate in the joints
The countries that forget we were all nomads
Love,
the language of which is forgotten
The pain of the unresolved conflicts that surround you,
but you didn't start

Oh this ! oh that ! all of a sudden, conscious ! you are in
the middle of !
Dear lord, make me forget how to please.
All this filth.
o sister, o brother, teach me that rap
All the pain that accumulates,
I want to spit them bars, puke that filth, I don't care if it
is to the void
Spill clear.
I want to no more please.

3

The choking pearl neck piece

The silence of the family (members)
Inside concrete buildings
Do you relate?
The distance of their worlds, while eating the same food
The desire and lack of control over each other
The unwantingly growing despise
The (un)understood values
The *how was your day* that waits to be asked till day
You don't know all that I suffered vs do you even know
what I go through
The fights and fights and fights of the past
The movies you never took each other to
The screams over normal chitchat
The arguments you are already into
The family's family that did you wrong
Some cousins you hold on to
I pray they all collapse
like a fallen pearl neck piece.

Freedom to you
Freedom to them
Amen.

4

Who fucked the emotional regulation in the fam?

Where did it all start?
One day or over the years,
You see a grandfather cannot be ever wrong, he is of
course
But you don't speak against a wild man
You might get angry onto him, but he is the bigger
drama king

I wonder why the father and the son don't speak heart to
heart!
It is the father's father who didn't begin.
When a generation is set to ruin, look into what the dead
didn't do
Many things a dead did right,
but it is what the dead didn't do that fuels
(a cycle that you desperately want to leave)

Angry, brave, entitled men nurtured by women.
Accepted over and over and over
Because of the norm.
It worked for many, it didn't for us.
You are gullible when you are young, it is too late when
the eyes open
A woman is trapped; to leave the chaos or stay for the
threads she has found!
What would I choose ! of course the freedom you'd think
Wrong,
often,
she ends up with a cheap bargain
To come out of trap requires you to go through many
others
Injured and blinded already, let me live with the threads I
have holded on, she'd choose.

No freedom for you, none for her
In the cycle of emotional dysregulation.

5

Freedom

When freedom is near
there is a deep sorrow,
there is music.

Attachment to the past and
her feelings don't want to leave.
They won't leave; it isn't possible,
but I move on to the Free.

I know there is one,
I feel it tonight.
I feel her free.
Surrounded with music, she is coming,
a new world is on her way.

6

Fifty Depressed Shades

The chaos of the mind
A never diagnosed switches of the brain
It is uncontrollable it seems,
I wonder what is real at times,
At the bottom of the failures I afloat
Unable to pinpoint a single thread to hold on

Chaos, Chaos, Chaos. I scream.
Cursed to die and live under the piles of the shambles of
the pressure
Press, press, pressureeee
(Thicha malai)
Press on me
(I secretly wish pito mujhe) (maybe death isn't that bad)

My mind, I'm sorry I don't want to blame on you
anymore
How tough it must be for you too.

On days, I cannot seem to do anything at all
Other than to succumb to the reality of my phone
and the bed
Unable to move an inch, or anything done
Is it the lack of trees?
Am I a prisoner of the concrete!
What are you seeking my brain!
What do I offer to this pain?

Years have passed, unliving my dreams
In the tunnel,
I call it the lifestyle of a worthless villain of the dark
When will the archetype change?

I succumb yet again, miles and miles in light years
At some moments, almost disappeared
My old friend makes sure to appear
Chaos, Chaos, Chaos, in my brain

A hundred and fifty shades of the pain.
Trembles in my brain.
I'm done, take me please the god of Medi—-effin—-tate!

7

The desire of death

The desire of death, I use to call it
It comes it goes, it stays, in longer and shorter span
to make you completely exhausted
to reach a point where nothing, nothing
but guilt, shame and humiliation survives.

Is it the death of vanity in disguise?

The involuntary desire of immolating in exhaustion
to chase self ruin
Sometimes it is substance, sometimes the reels
And sometimes it is the service to other
The goal of all if it is to just 'ruins' without rest (of the
mind).

That desire of death
Like something with life awaits the end of it, like a
breath; in and out, like the matchstick; bright then dusty
The inner omnipresent call (for growth and progress)
peeps like a creep
In the shadows, you beat yourself to punish.

There are hobbies that awaits,
new instruments the body seeks
Or forget all of that, I wish I just rested if nothing else.
But you cannot !
You cannot be left alone, something creeps in gently for
an eternity !
Is it
genetic?

What is it? The moon, the menstruation cycle!
The guilt of not changing the world ?
All the hate awaits to be expressed?
They all find their way, (through me!)

The desire for death however is not a wish to die
It is that slow revelation- of the self
(That one cannot hold on to for long)
It is in reality, the sticking; the sticking to yourself that is
tough
It is where the juice is,
but I am, I have been,
hardwired to (self) sabotage.
Stay.
Nani Stay. Stay here, in my body
I say to myself even though I'mma deep already onto my
knees in death.

It is not running to the substance or to the memes or any
other forms of the trade of the physical body
(for the temporary dopamine)
I sell my age or my eyes every other day
The running is real, the reason is fake.

It is the love for the self that I avoid.

Because sticking is to love
Accepting is to love
Bearing witness to the self- is love
The highest form of love- somehow I learned- to avoid
I am into the habit of leaving my body because the
environment wasn't safe.
It was never safe. So, I left and left and left.
Like decay, it rots when you leave it for too long.
But nothing, nothing is irreversible
Like despise
and hatred, joy is also just buried (waiting to reappear)

I left and left and left
now I have to learn to stay
-with me
and away from the desire of death.

8

River, where does she flow?

River,
where does she flow?

Where there is love
open sky,
forest,
birds and their friends,
where your sahelis are,
who follow happiness
who break the damns in their hearts
who go after the desires
who wander for a long long time
In their search,
rives flows
heaps and heaps of eternity.

9

The Dance of the Teej

Keeping the spirit high!
I dance tonight

moving my energy
living emotions,
twirling with it- like how they like to twirl with me,
how historical I think. They visited me in the depths of
the teej,
five oceans away.

Far away,
as a seed,
my being remembered!

- that I am supposed to move to the free.

Crying and crying and crying
and dancing and dancing and dancing
tearing down in laughter
being back the animal I am- my body remembers why
she came to me (during teej).

Tonight
I cried with my sisters
knowing deep in our hearts
knowing we are arriving near-
the farewell of us.
this departure is heart-fully felt.
We hugged all at once, for long, long and long.
Departures aren't planned but they happen.

Far away,
I remembered.
'The significance of the night in Nepal'
far in my land,
the festivity of my women
where I am from.

Teej ~ she arrives ~. on the new moon light
in all her darkness,
reminding
to make a new path
that the old has fallen
make a way
make a way
make way for the new.

So I dance.

10

Grateful to my rage

I will tear this land,
with my pain,
into the driest cracks and pieces like the drought does.
I will soak the ground I stand
with all my tears,
so moist
that you can fall deep into the pit of the earth,
if you slip into the land I pass.

I will grow
tallest, above the sky
with my fingers I shall squeeze
and crumble all the blue you see above.
Tall, giant,
my hair open,
I shall cross summits on my feet,
borders, bans and documents, I shall laugh upon.

Betrayals, robberies, taken for granted, stepped upon.
All,
I now remember.

Murderers of my innocence, listen.
The child is now free
but never to return to you.

Deserts and mountains, I shall crush fine into the grayest
powder
while screaming my lungs out-
They will become the loudest thunder ever.

I will rage
until the rage wants.

Because,
in the haze,
when nothing,
nothing was in control
rage came
to clear my pain.

11

Freedom from the feudal

Stars fell,
almost all nights they fell
But nevertheless
in the chaos of numbness
alone-
new dreams I braid.

I feared rest- immensely
I worshipped the ones who germinated fear.
The demon spoke-
"wait I will see u! It isn't enough"
"how did you not bring this, where is that?"
"where are all those resources you owe"

Infringed from my own
disguised in the lens of 'I am your people'
the feudal lords chase- I saw, when the masters didn't
find the slaves
as offerings, their own family bled.

I then, came clear.
Aimlessly wandered,
chopped and exhausted by my own people.

The dreams that others show you, are they ever yours?
I lost- all that was mine
was I ever mine? who all did I belong to?

I fell.
Down.
Then I came clear, late.

Aware.

Stars fell.
New dreams I braid- freedom from the feudal.
Freedom from the feudal.

12

I miss my unborn

To the unborn
who came to visit me in the dream
To the unborn
who got suppressed
under the pillars of the collective
What do I tell you?

Your need for recognition is justified.
The collective is a lot functional in your absence
if that helps
the foundations that crushed you definitely does
something
(not justice)

In dreams, you came alive
A healthy black born
with his great grandmother on his side, her long hair
open
You were happy and healthy.
In retrospection you mother is also getting there.

It would have happened!
If you were alive today, there would be absolute freedom.
But there is, you know too much gravity
of patriarchy and failed systems.
We have made heavy pillars on the ground
to hold a roof for many,
we live here, the collective of the privileged ones in their
limited space with limited norms.
The rest are unalived in fear.

But child I see you.
It is time to tell world the truth
that you were
once born,
and aborted in fear of stigmas, status and disgust of your
mother's collective.

But love - love is always in the air, before we were.
And the air - is changing.
Fast, erratically, killing us many
their system don't work, it never did
They killed you, and they try killing me.

I thought forgetting is enough
but it shall never be -

You Will Be Born.

Homes need rebuilding every era each day-
the fixed walls won't work on a round structure.
so we will take the pillars and throw it in the air to make
space
(nothing shall be oppressed anymore),
we will build you a floaty home that will fit you, let you
fly,
we will make what is called upon -

Freedom, Love, and Queerness.

(a home that fits you)
(a home that fits me)
(a home that changes but fits us together, in the same
world)
We will build you a home (in the same world)
My aborted child
I miss you.

13

On Crossing the Borders

Please tell me.
You know it already
you are going.
There is security (maybe) and certainty.
You have packed your bags.
Do not- not go because you do not know.
Nobody knows the future's future.
Nobody knew, nobody can.
It is better than to sit here - lose yourself in fear
The future's product - you cannot tell.
Somewhere inside of me I want to be beaten up, beaten
up badly and disabled so I don't go
somewhere inside of me,
I want to be caged and live a pathetic life
because some part of me has declared:
You are worthless to not have lived here
To not have tried hard enough
To have chosen the trees over people,
to have chosen the skirt over covering up

To have chosen to flee for the dream that I haven't
clearly seen (yet)
To flee for being a stranger again
To flee for not just one but many dreams that I do not
know if they are mirrages
Or maybe! I am just coping with the stress that isn't
enough this time (in leaving again)
So I add,
some more to it, making it the story of my pain!

Why not!
to be covered in stress was often the pattern, whether I
left or not
waiting always,
for a holiday to distress
but there are no holidays - for the ones who has no
structures to flow
No rhythms this time that isn't mine.
Remember the rituals here that didn't serve!
The other fascinating rituals that weren't mine.

What if I never wake up in real time to what I'm signing
up to!
Impossible.

My uncertainty speaks uncertainties to those around me

who care, and hence triggered
however it maybe
I hear them (or maybe it is just me),
'why do you want to fucking go?'
Because I came to leave one more time
to leave is the rightful rite given to me by my land -
Go, explore, be many, be in harmony says Nepal
Find you, find your craft, be the creative says the spirits.
Undo the hesitation
if you didn't want to leave, the hesitation wouldn't be
there in the first place
I feel the weight on my shoulders again
the more I stay the more weight it will gain, burying all
of me day by day
Like how it once did in an unfulfilling relationship you
committed to
which said, let me just play my part.

Too deep sunken, get out Nani
It is in actuality, the road to you, to be free
Choose you, choose you, choose you, choose you, choose
you, choose you, choose you
(once a witch said)
I choose me, now today
I am chasing the nomad in me, until I settle, just for me,
just for me,
I leave again.

14

Thank you and goodbye

A narrative that you live in
like that of a god:
pure, sinless, beautiful, bold
in the world of the norms that serve you
sorrounded by ideas of high morale ground
higher sacrifices, higher gratification.
All that you receive, all that you contribute,
all that you sacrifice.
Ah ! What an ideal you are !

Dear elder sister,
I wish your life was a little sinful, a little more exciting,
what are you secret indulgences ? Tell me,
How was your first sex?
I wish your difficulties were more than ideal,
I wish our conversations were more than ideal.
I wish at the end of the day, you tell me
Fuck it Sister !! fuck it all, fuck all of this.
"Live your life"

I wish. I long.

No, no. No disrespect.
I swear, by my heart that I live for - I love you, I do.
I see you, your achievements,
your way of care and shelter you provide,
the barriers you must have broken;
all these men and their systems,
so gracefully you rose above all, on top
dear sister, what a goddess you are,
a power Queen in the land of patriarchy- where I belong
too.

Secretly though, I wish, you saw-
how difficult it is for my heart to grow here,
in your land of patriarchy;
Ah ! what reforms we have now - in this land.
How lucky you must think I am, & I am
Thank you Queen, I bow.
and all other queens before you, all other sisters,
mothers,
the brothers who joined you.
Thank you.

But this heart of mine, dear sister
continues to weep,
a different land it seeks.

Your free world of high morale, it pains me.
It is not mine, it will not be mine.
& I run, maybe fly.

Bye Bye you wonderful woman
Goodbye,
See you later.

15

Frida Kahlo in my face

I carry the mustache of Frida Kahlo in my face
thin lines of hair I refuse to betray,
I travelled cities of my people and their neighbors
women they all had the same face (of hair).

Am I to be ashamed of this supposed recognition of
masculinity?
Did women take up so much so that they are slowly
turning into men?
Will I find a man who will unsee my insecurities?
Thank god I also like women (I believe women will see
me for who I am)
but where will I find them?

I carry the mustache of Frida Kahlo in my face.
I try to be proud every other day
Why are you lazy, just take it off, one day the guy
bestfriend said
I convince myself it isn't that long (yet)

PCOS PCOD Youtube screams, are you having abnormal
hairgorwth!
Have you tried the organic hair removal cream?
Turmeric, ginger, herbs and their various names.
I carry the mustache of Frida Kahlo in my face,
and in my body, my very own ancestral patches of thick
black remembrance.

16

The unforgotten longing

I have forgotten his face
so I will forget yours too.

But today '
is a tougher day,
today your smile walks all over me.

One day, you will be forgotten
but today the longing for you aches me and my heart,

You ! Be forgotten soon.
Be gone soon, I cannot say.
The heart, she aches for you
There is some magic to do
some voodoo to uncover

And, I am trapped
in between *my heart* and *my knowing*.
With the craving,

longing and the distance came
so we have reached only far apart far away
-reminding me of my parents' love
always longing, always away.

But hey!
beautiful things can be grown under their roof too.
(look at me !)
so do I dream one
(home)
with you too?

Let me listen to you more
the next time
(if there is one!)
most part of me has given up,
but that one bit
keeps craving you
and your beauty
so the next time (please let there be one)
I will listen to you more
the next time,
keeping myself intact,
relaxed and tuned into you gently
will you let me?

17

That abstract painting

It all mixes up in the farthest planet
I found out!

I often wait;
then logic follows- all that feels.
(a busy mind)
It is that time of the month,
I will bury you:

one more time.

I let you peek,
because your butterfly eyes shine vibrant opaque,

the wait for exhaustion
is the wait for the sleep,
tonight also,
I long for tomorrow (night).

I repeat (I'm)
with little hope (never hopelessness)

all that I do- I don't surrender
(fully)
because numbness is no longer home
(not always the case)
but more so of a passing guest (these days).

& one (fine) day will come
I will get

a(LLLLLLLLLLLL) the sleep
-I want,

(my moon), she promised me,

18

Justice

Justice is a bright burning star
it heals you..
in ways,
that makes it easier for the heart to forgive.

19

I was an insect

में कीड़ा हूँ
में कीड़ा थी
मुझे कीड़ा होनेकी चेतना हमेशा रहेंगी

I am in insect
I was an insect
The memory of 'being' from an insect shall live forever.

As an advanced insect,
I shall wear clothes.
Under these textiles, my bare body resembles the
crawling insect
doesn't it? Imagine me,
if I crawl naked
on the floor
I am as fragile as a cabbage pest.

I am also a dog
I would like to sniff
your genitalia
My boobs sag like that of a bitch

if I kneel down
on these four legs.

I'd sniff you,
you, you, and you
all of you, freely
regardless of what our ties are.

But now, I have to pretend
that touching you is a sin
and touching me isn't allowed
that I cannot howl
my two legs are now hands
and my body is upright
forced to etiquettes.

I can no more sniff,
If I do, it is very few of you,
mostly one at a time with a contract.
We play with fire and ingredients, call it a marriage
or sometimes casually get a partner, or boyfriend or a
girl,
who I shall be allowed to be in bed with
they I will smell with all my rights,
like a dog!
the armpits,
are my favorite.

But, nonetheless
the memory shall live
that I was
and will be
once an insect, a dog,
and a degenerate?

20

My kind heart is stubborn

Let me dance the dance
Let me sing my song
Let me,
fuel my fire
Let me,
nourish my soul
Let me be kind to me.

I shall bring peace down to my feet.

Dear me,
Rest, Pause, Go, Rest
Pause, Go, Rest, Pause.

Dear me,
I love you baby
You can what you want.

21

A King in us

A king in me rises
when governments fail.

When people cry, fallen prey in the hands of corporates
and guns, pimped by their own voted ones.
when the meaning of civilization is forgotten,
when governments sell everything to the merchants,
who is prosperity for when more than half of your
people are drained?
who is the bikas for when you decide for them?

There is a king in us
who remembers the essence
of the deed of the treaty,
the ruler and the people had.

A king in victory doesn't harm the opponent's subject
A king seeks the blessings of the goddesses of the new
territory
A king recognizes an emperor and keeps it away.
A king doesn't divide the people, a king is amongst them.

A king worries if the subjects are fed.
The ancestors of the king has seen many, many wars and
neglect.
A king today unites and desires peace.

A king renounces weapons of mass destruction.
A king is trained to see the greed.
A king sees the dances of the devil.
A king calls to celebrate so the joy of the people keeps
off the leeches in the collectives.

A king is the thread of the garland.

A king's legacy is not a king's child, it is another
brilliant, kind leader.
A king's legacy shines bright in the laughter of women
and their grandchildren.
A king's legacy is in the language of the art that has
flourished without boundaries.
Absence of conflict is not a king's legacy, but is a culture
of embracing it; that gives rise to the diversities.

Poets and revolutionaries find glimpses of changes in
their homes.
A king's anger is never to the critics.
A king knows to retire.
A king understands power and is not undertaken by it.

The power rests in a king when a king is split and two
women in love come out of the king's beheaded head
who drink the spurted blood from the neck promising to
behead the decay in the king's surrounding.
A king isn't only political or just religious.
Out of all things possible, a king is first of the people.

I wonder who the government is?